# CLASSIC *f*M

# THE
# WEDDING
# COLLECTION

## BEAUTIFUL WEDDING MUSIC
## ARRANGED FOR PIANO SOLO

**FABER *ff* MUSIC**

# Contents

Arranged by Pam Wedgwood

Faber Music in association with Classic FM, a Global Radio station.
Faber Music is the exclusive print publisher for all Global Radio sheet music product.

© 2011 Faber Music Ltd
First published in 2011 by Faber Music Ltd
Bloomsbury House 74–77 Great Russell Street London WC1B 3DA
Music processed by Jackie Leigh
Cover design by Sue Clarke
Printed in England by Caligraving Ltd
All rights reserved

ISBN10: 0-571-53614-X
EAN13: 978-0-571-53614-6

To buy Faber Music/Global Radio publications, or to find out about the full range of titles available,
please contact your local retailer, or go to www.fabermusic.com or www.classicfm.com/shop.
For sales enquiries, contact Faber Music at sales@fabermusic.com or tel: +44(0)1279 828982.

# Foreword

With so much to plan for a wedding day, choosing the perfect music will go a long way to making the event memorable and special. You may find that some of these pieces will be suitable for either a church or civil ceremony, but please note that civil ceremonies usually don't allow the playing of pieces with religious elements.

For the arrival of the bride, there are some very famous options to choose from, each with unmistakable melodies. Wagner's **Bridal Chorus**, from his masterwork **Lohengrin** is always popular, and Clarke's **The Prince of Denmark's March** has become a processional classic. The hugely popular Pachelbel's **Canon** is perfect for civil ceremonies, and arguably the most famous wedding processional of all, Mendelssohn's **Wedding March** from 'A Midsummer Night's Dream' will add a Shakespearian touch.

The signing of the registers is a natural opportunity for music to be played. Bach's **Jesu, Joy of Man's Desiring** includes a devotional chorale melody, perfect for church ceremonies, or you could consider Howard Goodall's setting of **Psalm 23: The Lord is My Shepherd**. For civil ceremonies, Elgar's **Salut d'amour** and Debussy's **Clair de lune** are both beautiful choices, as is Shostakovich's **Romance** from his 1955 film score of 'The Gadfly'. Lovland's **You Raise Me Up** is also a hugely popular and uplifting choice.

With the ceremony concluded, you may like to choose something celebratory for the happy couple – how about Handel's **La Rejouissance** from 'Music for the Royal Fireworks', or Purcell's **Trumpet Tune**.

# Wedding March
from *A Midsummer Night's Dream*

Felix Mendelssohn

# Bridal Chorus
## from *Lohengrin*

Richard Wagner

# Trumpet Tune

Henry Purcell

# The Prince of Denmark's March

Jeremiah Clarke

# Canon

Johann Pachelbel

# La Rejouissance

## from *Music for the Royal Fireworks*

George Frideric Handel

**Allegro moderato, con spirito**

# Clair de lune

Claude Debussy

# Panis Angelicus

César Franck

# Ave Maria

Charles Gounod / J.S. Bach

# The Lord is My Shepherd
## Psalm 23

Howard Goodall
Arranged by Alan Gout

D.S. al ⊕
then to Coda

CODA

rall.

# Jerusalem

Hubert Parry

**Slow, with movement**

# Salut d'Amour

Edward Elgar

# Jesu, Joy of Man's Desiring

Johann Sebastian Bach

# Air on the G String

Johann Sebastian Bach

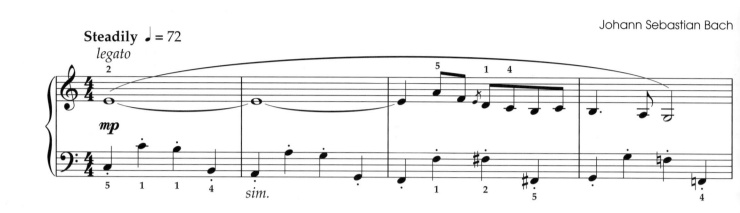

# Romance

from *The Gadfly*

Dmitri Shostakovich

# You Raise Me Up

Words and Music by
Rolf Lovland and Brendan Graham

# I Was Glad

Hubert Parry

# ALSO AVAILABLE
# FROM FABER MUSIC AND
# CLASSIC *f*M

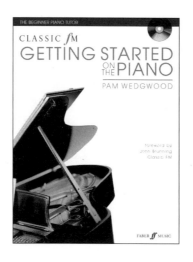

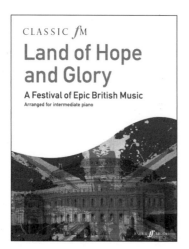

To buy Faber Music publications or to find out about the full range of titles available
please contact your local music retailer or Faber Music sales enquiries:

Faber Music Ltd, Burnt Mill, Elizabeth Way, Harlow CM20 2HX
Tel: +44 (0) 1279 82 89 82   Fax: +44 (0) 1279 82 89 83
sales@fabermusic.com   fabermusic.com   expressprintmusic.com